No. 38

FRED BASSET

by GRAHAM

PUBLISHED BY ASSOCIATED MAGAZINES LTD
FOR MAIL NEWSPAPERS GROUP plc.

© 1986 MAIL NEWSPAPERS GROUP plc.

ISBN 0 85144 363 X

DISTRIBUTION BY: Seymour Press, 334 Brixton Road, London SW9 7AG
Tel: 01-733-4444 Telex: 88-12945

PRINTED BY CHASE WEB OFFSET, PLYMOUTH

19/5 GRAHAM

FRED BASSET

by Alex Graham

FRED BASSET

by Alex Graham

FRED BASSET

by Alex Graham

One of these vital services doesn't cost Government a penny.

The Police, the Fire Brigade and the Ambulance Service are all financed entirely by Central and Local Government.

The exception is the RSPCA. It is in fact a Charity, funded mainly by the legacies of caring individuals.

Sadly, there are many who don't realise that the RSPCA receives no State Aid. Perhaps the misconception stems from the uniform worn by our National force of over 200 full-time Inspectors.

Or perhaps because we are often seen working closely with the Police in securing animal cruelty convictions – 2,112 last year alone. Or perhaps it's the fact that like other

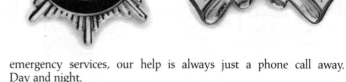

emergency services, our help is always just a phone call away. Day and night.

But if you're thinking that this is a plea for Government support, don't worry. It isn't.

The RSPCA is happy to remain a Charity, so long as enough people remember.

If you would like a brochure detailing the work of the RSPCA, and information on making legacies and covenants, write to the Society's Solicitor at RSPCA, Causeway, Horsham, Sussex RH12 1HG.

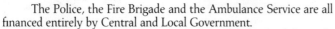

Charity in Action

FRED BASSET

by Alex Graham

FRED BASSET

by Alex Graham

HOW COULD YOU?

YOU'RE JUST NOT TO BE TRUSTED.

I LEAVE THE ROOM FOR A LITTLE WHILE, AND WHAT HAPPENS?

YOU EAT A WHOLE HALF-POUND BOX OF CHOCOLATES!

IT'S NOT FAIR!... I LIKE CHOCOLATES TOO, YOU KNOW.

SORRY! YOU KNOW HOW IT IS... I HAD ONE...THEN ANOTHER...

For once, it's not me who's getting into trouble.

30/6

GRAHAM

FRED BASSET
by Alex Graham

7/7 Graham

FRED BASSET

by Alex Graham

FRED BASSET
by GRAHAM

5961

...AND THIS IS FRED. AT FOUR MONTHS

ADORABLE

WHAT A PITY HE HAD TO GROW UP

We resent that, don't we?

© Associated Newspapers Group p.l.c., 1982

FRED BASSET
by GRAHAM

HE'S STARTED!

COME ON! HE'LL BE ALL RIGHT

On principle, I always make a protest when they go out!

© Associated Newspapers Group p.l.c., 1982

5962

HE'LL SETTLE DOWN ONCE WE'VE GONE

Too right, I will!

FRED BASSET

by Alex Graham

FRED BASSET

by Alex Graham

11/8

GRAHAM

FRED BASSET

by Alex Graham

FRED BASSET

by Alex Graham

We're in a very dangerous situation here...

Deep in enemy territory.

There's a bull terrier that rules the roost here...

...and you never know when he's going to pounce.

That's why I've put my scouts out.

8/9

FRED BASSET

by Alex Graham

FRED BASSET

by Alex Graham

FRED BASSET

by Alex Graham

I never get bored on the beach—always plenty to do.

I've just had a dip in the sea...

...before that a jog along the beach...

..chased a seagull or two...

...and now I'm building a sand castle!

Graham 29/9

FRED BASSET
by GRAHAM
5973

It's no use appealing to me, lad....It was a perfectly fair shoulder charge!

© Associated Newspapers Group p.l.c., 1982

FRED BASSET
by GRAHAM
5978

FETCH IT!

Here we go again! Backwards and forwards!

It's so BORING!

I think he thinks that I enjoy it....

FETCH IT!

© Associated Newspapers Group p.l.c., 1982

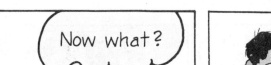

FRED BASSET

by Alex Graham

FRED BASSET

by Alex Graham

The trouble with my breed is that if I get a scent...

...I immediately begin to bark...

...alarming the quarry, which sets off at high speed...

...leaving me far behind!

So, I never catch anything!

If you're a Basset hound, you can't win!

20/10 GRAHAM

FOUNDED 1891

NCDL

NATIONAL CANINE DEFENCE LEAGUE

The antics of Fred Basset are a joy to read but the plight of the many thousands of homeless dogs bring tears to our eyes.

Please support the National Canine Defence League, Britain's leading Charity that really cares for stray, abandoned and unwanted dogs.

Fourteen Centres are maintained to give shelter to the cast out members of our canine society. No healthy dog is ever destroyed.

Please will you help us to do more?

Further details from: Dept FB
National Canine Defence League
1 Pratt Mews
London
NW1 0AD

FRED BASSET

by Alex Graham

FRED BASSET

by Alex Graham

HELLO, SID! GOOD, YOU'VE BROUGHT YOUR TROMBONE.

Trombone?

PETER'S COMING BY LATER WITH HIS DRUMS...

Drums?

...AND CHARLIE'S PROMISED TO BRING HIS BASS GUITAR.

Bass guitar?

I'VE BEEN PRACTISING MY PIANO PART.

I don't know where we're going, but we're off!

10/11
GRAHAM

FRED BASSET

by Alex Graham

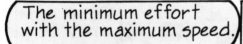

27/10 GRAHAM

FRED BASSET
by GRAHAM

5991

He's home!

FRED BASSET
by GRAHAM

A CREAMY TOFFEE BAR TOPPED WITH CHOPPED ALMONDS AND JUICY CHERRIES...

5992

...A LAYER OF MOUTH-WATERING FUDGE...

...SMOTHERED IN RICH, DARK SMOOTH CHOCOLATE

She's on a diet...

FRED, HOW COULD YOU...

HOW COULD YOU GO INTO THE LARDER AND STEAL THOSE STEAKS?

THEY WERE A SPECIAL TREAT FOR DINNER TONIGHT.

NOW I SUPPOSE I'LL HAVE TO OPEN A CAN OF SOMETHING

IT'S SO DISAPPOINTING.

When she puts it like that, I feel like such a heel!

1/12
GRAHAM

I COULD CRY!

I'd much rather she had given me a good clout and got it over with.

FRED BASSET by GRAHAM

HOW CAN I GET TO SLEEP WITH YOU SNORING AWAY DOWN HERE!

6001

Now I'll never get off!

Especially now that HE'S started!

FRED BASSET by GRAHAM

I'm EXHAUSTED!.... If he doesn't nip up this tree I'll have to give up

6002

Good! He has! That's a relief!

So I didn't have to lose face...

FRED BASSET

by Alex Graham

I WONDER IF ANYONE CAME BY OR CALLED WHILE WE WERE OUT.

No! Nothing like that.

But there were mysterious creakings upstairs...

What sounded like heavy breathing in the hall..

Odd, whistling noises coming down the chimney...

The tap-tap of ghostly fingers at the window.

Just the usual noises I hear when they're out and I'm left on my own.

12/1

GRAHAM

FRED BASSET
by GRAHAM

Perfect condition... lovingly cared for... fault free... low mileage... one owner...

6009

POST OFFICE

STILL ONLY 37½ p

And now fully licensed for another year....

© Associated Newspapers Group p.l.c., 1983

FRED BASSET
by GRAHAM

Sausages!... There for the taking!

6010

And I can't resist them, being a natural thief

Pity!... I was trying to go straight!

© Associated Newspapers Group p.l.c., 1983

FRED BASSET
by GRAHAM

He could lead the six of clubs from his own hand, ruff it in dummy and cash in the diamonds. Alternatively, he could play the King of hearts and hope the Queen will drop, making his ten.....

6011.

*Or he could lead a **small** heart, try the finesse, and if it comes off draw the trumps..... But they may be unevenly distributed, and then they could run away with their clubs if they got in*

*Frankly, I'm glad **I'm** not playing this hand*

© Associated Newspapers Group p.l.c. 1983

FRED BASSET
by GRAHAM

6012

QUIET! I wish he wouldn't make this noise at breakfast

I can't hear the television for the crackle of his Krispipops!

© Associated Newspapers Group p.l.c. 1983

FRED BASSET

by Alex Graham

FRED BASSET `6021`
by GRAHAM

She's having a ladies' coffee party, so I'm banished to the kitchen!

Because of what happened last time, I suppose

With all the chatter that was going on, nobody spotted me at the shortbread fingers

FRED BASSET `6022`
by GRAHAM

NO!... NO WALK THIS EVENING!

No?

We'll see about that!

FRED WANTS A WALK

It never fails....

FRED BASSET

by Alex Graham

CHECK

That sudden flurry of activity has left me quite breathless with excitement

COMING!

There was this terrible scream from the kitchen.

WHAT HAPPENED?

I HAD A SHOCK FROM THE ELECTRIC IRON.

BRANDY!...A DROP OF BRANDY!

JUST THE THING TO SETTLE THE NERVES AFTER AN EXPERIENCE LIKE THAT.

I could see he'd had a nasty fright...

23/2

GRAHAM